Go

By Ian Ansdell

PUBLISHING

WRITING *to* REMEMBER

WRITING *to* REMEMBER

79 Main Street, Newtongrange,
Midlothian EH22 4NA
Tel: 0131 344 0414   Fax: 0845 075 6085
E-mail: info@lang-syne.co.uk
www.langsyneshop.co.uk

Design by Dorothy Meikle
Printed by Printwell Ltd
© Lang Syne Publishers Ltd 2022

ISBN 978-1-85217-234-3

Gordon

SEPT NAMES INCLUDE:

Adam	Culane	Jupp
Adams	Darg	Lawrie
Adamson	Darge	Mallett
Addie	Edison	Mavor
Adie	Eddie	Mill
Addison	Edie	Mills
Aitken	Gardiner	Miline
Atkin	Gardner	Milne
Atkinson	Huntley	Morrice
Connon	Huntly	Teall
Cromb	Jessiman	Todd
Cullen	Jopp	

Gordon

MOTTO:
Bydand (Abiding).

SLOGAN:
"A Gordon! A Gordon!"

CREST:
A stag's head above a coronet.

PLANT BADGE:
Rock ivy.

TERRITORY:
Strathbogie, The Merse, Deeside.

Chapter one:

The origins of the clan system

by Rennie McOwan

The original Scottish clans of the Highlands and the great families of the Lowlands and Borders were gatherings of families, relatives, allies and neighbours for mutual protection against rivals or invaders.

Scotland experienced invasion from the Vikings, the Romans and English armies from the south. The Norman invasion of what is now England also had an influence on land-holding in Scotland. Some of these invaders stayed on and in time became 'Scottish'.

The word clan derives from the Gaelic language term 'clann', meaning children, and it was first used many centuries ago as communities were formed around tribal lands in glens and mountain fastnesses.

The format of clans changed over the centuries, but at its best the chief and his family held the land on behalf of all, like trustees, and the ordinary clansmen and women believed they had a blood relationship with the founder of their clan.

There were two way duties and obligations. An inadequate chief could be deposed and replaced by someone of greater ability.

Clan people had an immense pride in race. Their relationship with the chief was like adult children to a father and they had a real dignity.

The concept of clanship is very old and a more feudal notion of authority gradually crept in.

Pictland, for instance, was divided into seven principalities ruled by feudal leaders who were the strongest and most charismatic leaders of their particular groups.

By the sixth century the 'British' kingdoms of Strathclyde, Lothian and Celtic Dalriada (Argyll) had emerged and Scotland, as one nation, began to take shape in the time of King Kenneth MacAlpin.

Some chiefs claimed descent from

ancient kings which may not have been accurate in every case.

By the twelfth and thirteenth centuries the clans and families were more strongly brought under the central control of Scottish monarchs.

Lands were awarded and administered more and more under royal favour, yet the power of the area clan chiefs was still very great.

The long wars to ensure Scotland's independence against the expansionist ideas of English monarchs extended the influence of some clans and reduced the lands of others.

Those who supported Scotland's greatest king, Robert the Bruce, were awarded the territories of the families who had opposed his claim to the Scottish throne.

In the Scottish Borders country – the notorious Debatable Lands – the great families built up a ferocious reputation for providing warlike men accustomed to raiding into England and occasionally fighting one another.

Chiefs had the power to dispense justice and to confiscate lands and clan warfare produced a society where martial virtues – courage, hardiness, tenacity – were greatly admired.

Gradually the relationship between the clans and the Crown became strained as Scottish monarchs became more orientated to life in the Lowlands and, on occasion, towards England.

The Highland clans spoke a different language, Gaelic, whereas the language of Lowland Scotland and the court was Scots and in more modern times, English.

Highlanders dressed differently, had different customs, and their wild mountain land sometimes seemed almost foreign to people living in the Lowlands.

It must be emphasised that Gaelic culture was very rich and story-telling, poetry, piping, the clarsach (harp) and other music all flourished and were greatly respected.

Highland culture was different from other parts of Scotland but it was not inferior or less sophisticated.

Central Government, whether in London or Edinburgh, sometimes saw the Gaelic clans as

*"The spirit of the clan means much
to thousands of people"*

a challenge to their authority and some sent expeditions into the Highlands and west to crush the power of the Lords of the Isles.

Nevertheless, when the eighteenth century Jacobite Risings came along the cause of the Stuarts was mainly supported by Highland clans.

The word Jacobite comes from the Latin for James – Jacobus. The Jacobites wanted to restore the exiled Stuarts to the throne of Britain.

The monarchies of Scotland and England became one in 1603 when King James VI of Scotland (1st of England) gained the English throne after Queen Elizabeth died.

The Union of Parliaments of Scotland and England, the Treaty of Union, took place in 1707.

Some Highland clans, of course, and Lowland families opposed the Jacobites and supported the incoming Hanoverians.

After the Jacobite cause finally went down at Culloden in 1746 a kind of ethnic cleansing took place. The power of the chiefs was curtailed. Tartan and the pipes were banned in law.

Many emigrated, some because they

wanted to, some because they were evicted by force. In addition, many Highlanders left for the cities of the south to seek work.

Many of the clan lands became home to sheep and deer shooting estates.

But the warlike traditions of the clans and the great Lowland and Border families lived on, with their descendants fighting bravely for freedom in two world wars.

Remember the men from whence you came, says the Gaelic proverb, and to that could be added the role of many heroic women.

The spirit of the clan, of having roots, whether Highland or Lowland, means much to thousands of people.

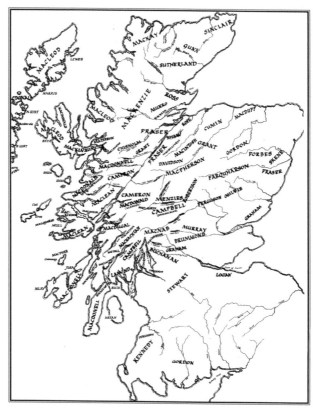

A map of the clans' homelands

Chapter two:

In the beginning...

What's in a name? In the case of Gordon, its meaning and origin are far from clear.

Some say it derives from a Berwickshire placename – 'gor-dun', meaning hill fort – while according to other accounts the clan's ancestor came from Gourdon in France around the time of the Norman Conquest.

A third, and more fanciful, theory reaches back to a city of Macedonia called Gordonia.

Whatever the truth, the Berwickshire connection certainly becomes clearer as written accounts begin in the twelfth century, showing that between 1150 and 1160 one Richard de Gordon granted land to the monks of Kelso.

And the clan's story truly comes to life with the arrival of Richard's great-great-grandson, Sir Adam de Gordon.

Like many ancient and noble families, the Gordons' fortune hinged on being on the right side in times of strife. When the Scots lost the battle of Falkirk in 1298 and William Wallace was taken off by the English to his eventual execution, the Guardianship of Scotland fell to two men - Robert the Bruce and John Comyn.

Almost inevitably they fell out. Their animosity continued through Edward I's conquest of Scotland, and culminated in 1306 when Bruce cut down John 'The Red' Comyn with his sword before the high altar of Greyfriars Kirk in Dumfries. Bruce was excommunicated and outlawed for this sacriligious act, and civil war followed.

Adam de Gordon had been one of Comyn's supporters and joined Edward of England in vengeful pursuit of Bruce. But after Edward's death, an English Border commander made the mistake of plundering Gordon lands in Berwickshire and even imprisoning Adam, who promptly switched sides, pleading with the Pope to end Bruce's excommunication and serving Bruce faithfully after he became king.

Later, in 1320, Adam was to claim a glittering place in the nation's history by carrying to Rome the historic Declaration of Arbroath, which sought the Pope's support in establishing the independence of Scotland from its southern neighbour.

*The quarrel between Comyn
and Robert the Bruce*

Chapter three:

The move north

Adam de Gordon's loyalty to Robert the Bruce brought him rich rewards in the shape of extensive estates in Strathbogie in Aberdeenshire.

These had formerly been owned by David of Strathbolgyn, chief of Clan MacDuff, who had turned against the Scottish king just before Bannockburn.

Sir Adam gave his new lands the name of Huntly, after a village in Gordon parish, and is believed to have married a daughter of Strathbolgyn.

Sadly, these were troubled times and the family's ascendancy brought little relief from the savagery of war. Sir Adam himself was killed in 1333 while fighting the English at the battle of Halidon Hill - ironically in Berwickshire.

In 1376 his great-grandson, Sir John Gordon, had the family's ownership of

Strathbogie confirmed in a charter from King Robert II but was killed at the battle of Otterburn in 1388, when the Scots defeated an army led by Henry 'Hotspur' Percy, son of the earl of Northumberland. John's son Adam also fell in battle at Homildon in 1402.

With Adam's death, the old Gordon line continued through the Gordons of Lochinvar in Galloway, who later became the Viscounts of Kenmure.

However, the chieftainship was passed on through Adam's Elizabeth, whose husband, Sir Alexander Seton, is named as Lord Gordon in a document of 1429 and whose son Alexander became Earl of Huntly in 1455.

This line continued the Gordons' position as one of Scotland's leading families for nearly 400 years, with the 6th Earl becoming Marquis in 1599 and the 9th Earl created Duke in 1684.

However, the dukedom became extinct in 1836 when the 5th Duke died without a male heir, and a distant cousin succeeded as Earl and Marquis.

So prominent was the family that in their day the Dukes of Gordon were called 'The Cock of the North'. Their most ancient title, however, was 'Gudeman of the Bog' after the Bog-of-Gight in the Banffshire parish of Bellie.

Battle of Halidon Hill

Chapter four:

Dark days at Huntly Castle

In the meantime, the Gordon's famous stronghold of Huntly Castle – sometimes called Strathbogie – saw more than its fair share of the ebb and flow of Scotland's turbulent history.

In 1452 the first Earl of Huntly led the royal army against the Douglases. But while he triumphed at the battle of Brechin, his neighbour the Earl of Moray was busy burning down the wooden castle built by one of the Strathbolgyns in the twelfth century.

After punishing the raiders, the Earl embarked on the great work of building Huntly Castle, a task completed by his son. At its heart is an enormous keep, with a large round tower at the south west corner. The new castle became a magnet for the great and the good.

In 1496 Perkin Warbeck, who claimed the English throne of Henry VII, married Lady Catherine Gordon there in the presence of the Scottish king.

When Perkin's challenge ended in execution in 1498, Catherine was treated kindly by Henry. She stayed in England, remarried and became known there as the White Rose of Scotland.

By the period of the fourth Earl, fashions had changed. He thought the castle was gloomy, but when his substantial rebuilding during the early 1550s was finished, it was recognised as the finest house in Scotland. But then came the wars of religion.

In 1594, during the reign of James IV, Huntly was accused along with the Earls of Angus and Errol of conspiring with the King of Spain to restore the Roman Catholic religion in Scotland.

After an army of 1,500 men led by Huntly and Errol defeated a force of 5,000 commanded by the Earl of Argyll at Glenlivet, the King was forced by the Protestant nobles to lead an army into the north. James prevailed, and much of Huntly Castle was destroyed.

In keeping with the shifting alliances of the time, it was only two years before the Earl was back in the King's favour to the extent that James created him the first Marquess of Huntly.

The castle's magnificence was restored along with that of the family - only for both to face ruin once more through the devotion of George, the second Marquess, to Charles I.

In 1638, George refused to subscribe to the Protestants' National Covenant, and was driven from Strathbogie by the Marquess of Montrose. George was captured and taken to Edinburgh, where he was declared an outlaw and excommunicated.

Seven years later along with Montrose, who by this time had changed sides, he took Aberdeen for the Royalists and later raised forces for Charles I in the north. But the tide was against him. George was captured, and beheaded in Edinburgh by the Covenanters in 1649.

The Covenanters sacked Huntly Castle and after the Civil War it was never again occupied by the family.

Left to rack and ruin, it became little more than a quarry and dumping ground until 1923 when the government took it over to preserve a vital part of Scotland's heritage.

The Covenanters

Chapter five:

Sealed with a kiss

The second Duke of Gordon, Alexander, while Marquess of Huntly, came out for the 'Old Pretender' in the first Jacobite uprising in 1715 and fought at the Battle of Sheriffmuir, but later received a pardon and eventually succeeded to the Dukedom in 1716.

William, Viscount of Kenmure, head of the Border Gordons, was less fortunate. As Jacobite commander in southern Scotland before defeat at Preston, he was executed on Tower Hill.

Alexander's eldest son, Cosmo George, headed the house during the Jacobite Rebellion of 1745. As a Protestant he did not join the Rising but his uncle, Lord Lewis Gordon, led a strong force of clansmen in support of Bonnie Prince Charlie before defeat at Culloden.

Thereafter, like most Highland families, the Gordons settled into respectable Britishness.

The clan name was carried brilliantly forward not by its heads but by its regiment.

The Gordon Highlanders was raised in 1794 by the fourth Duke of Gordon as a regiment of Highland Foot (infantry) to serve in the French Revolutionary Wars. Many of the original recruits were drawn from the Gordon estates, and the recruiting effort was assisted by the Duchess of Gordon, who is said to have offered a kiss, sealed with a one guinea coin, as an incentive to join up.

They saw action against France at Egmont-op-Zee in Holland in 1799, in the Egyptian expedition of 1801 and in the drawn-out Peninsular War in Spain, before playing a prominent part in the vanquishing of Napoleon at Quatre Bras and Waterloo in 1815.

The expansion of the British Empire as the nineteenth century progressed saw the Gordons serve on the frontiers of India, in Egypt, the Sudan and South Africa. Their extraordinary exploits included taking only 23 days to march 320 miles of mountainous territory between

The Duchess placed a guinea between her
lips and kissed each man as he joined up

Kabul and Kandahar in 1880 during the Second Afghan War, and a famous victory on the heights of Dargai, on India's North West Frontier, in 1897.

Around 50,000 Gordons saw service during the First World War and more than half were killed or wounded. In the Second World War, Gordon battalions served with the British Expeditionary Force in France in 1940, and in the Far East in 1942. They fought in the North Africa campaign, in Sicily and Italy, in the invasion of Europe and the liberation of Burma.

In the years after 1945, the Regiment took part in peace-keeping and anti-terrorist operations in Malaya, Borneo, Cyprus, Germany and Northern Ireland, with detachments serving in the Gulf War and Bosnia. In 1994, the regiment was amalgamated with the Seaforth, Gordons and Camerons to form the new Highland Regiment.

Chapter six:

Gutsy and gallant

Gordon was the 50th most frequent surname lodged at the General Register Office in 1995, and such a large family is also a clan of characters.

In the 1600s Robert Gordon of Straloch and his son James, the minister at Rothiemay, published Timothy Pont's early maps of Scotland and carried out detailed surveys of Edinburgh and Aberdeen.

Others sought out new territories. Patrick Gordon of Auchintoul (1635-99) was one of the foremost commanders of Peter the Great of Russia.

Alexander Gordon of Auchintoul, who lived from 1669 to 1751, was a general in the Russian army before returning to Scotland in 1711 and commanding part of the Jacobite army in the 1715 rising.

Robert Gordon (1665-1732) was an

Aberdeen merchant who traded so successfully
with the Baltic area that he was able to leave a
fortune to found a charity for educating boys in
the city. Robert Gordon University is now a proud
part of Aberdeen's educational establishment.

Rather more turbulent was Lord George
Gordon, who served in the Navy and in
Parliament before becoming the notorious leader
of a 50,000 strong mob in the five-day long No-
Popery Riots in London in 1780.

Tried for high treason but found not guilty,
he later adopted the Jewish faith and eventually
died in Newgate Gaol. One commentary says of
him kindly that he was "occasionally subject to
aberrations of intellect".

One of the most famous Gordons, though
seldom called by his full name, was Lord George
Gordon Byron. The Romantic poet, satirist, lover
and rake was born in poor surroundings in
Aberdeen, the son of Captain John Byron and
Catherine Gordon of Gight, before inheriting title
and property from a great-uncle.

Finally, no account of the clan would be

complete without mention of the Gay Gordons, the phrase describing the family which was later applied to the famous country dance.

The 'gay' does not mean merry but is a corruption of 'gey', meaning gallant, spirited and gutsy – or overwhelming and self-important.

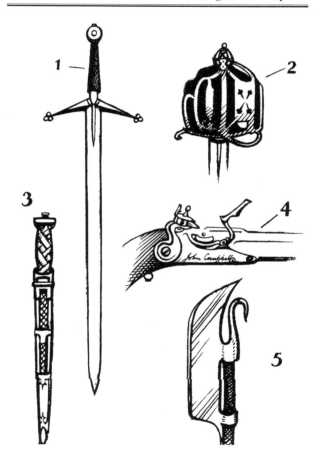

Highland weapons

1)   The claymore or two-handed sword
(fifteenth or early sixteenth century)

2)   Basket hilt of broadsword
made in Stirling, 1716

3)   Highland dirk
(eighteenth century)

4)   Steel pistol *(detail)* made in Doune

5)   Head of Lochaber Axe as carried
in the '45 and earlier